ALLIES

ALLIES

GREAT U.S. AND RUSSIAN
WORLD WAR II PHOTOGRAPHS

Introductions by

Grigori Chudakov and David E. Scherman

HUGH LAUTER LEVIN ASSOCIATES, INC., NEW YORK

Distributed by Macmillan Publishing Company, New York

© 1989 Hugh Lauter Levin Associates, Inc.

Introduction by Grigory Chudakov and Soviet photographs © 1989 Grigory Chudakov

Translation from the Russian by Todd Bludeau.

Produced by Mandarin Offset/
Printed and Bound in Hong Kong

ISBN 0-88363-389-2

Designed by Philip Grushkin

War at Close Range

by Grigori Chudakov

It has been said that wars are not photographed for history. War lives for the present, the minute, the second. Those who photograph war do not see into the future or think about what impressions their pictures of military reportage will have on their descendants. God forbid that the camera and its user should not escape in the moment of snapping a picture, for "war is not photographed from a distance, war can only be photographed at close range." These words belong to Konstantin Simonov, the famous Soviet journalist and writer of novels, novellas, and reportage on World War II. Giving his colleagues, photo- and film journalists, their due, he claimed that "it was even more difficult for war photocorrespondents and film operators to capture the war than it was for us to write about it."

Perhaps it is true that the war was not photographed for history, and yet we are completely justified in calling the photojournalists of World War II photochroniclers and their reportage a documentary witness without which it would be impossible to imagine the war's cruel face.

Soviet citizens, of whom twenty million gave their lives in those difficult years, called the war against fascist Germany the Great Patriotic War. For them it was "Great" not only in its scale, but also in the high moral duty it demanded of all humanity, threatened by fascist enslavement. It was "Patriotic" insofar as it involved the defense of the Motherland, the multinational Fatherland, and the social gains of the Soviet people.

Who are they, the photochroniclers of the Great Patriotic War? What place do they occupy in the rich and illustrious history of Soviet photojournalism and photographic arts?

The most famous were known by their photographs in illustrated publications and photography exhibitions of prewar Soviet Russia. An unprecedented flight in culture and art, spawned by the October Revolution, gave not only Eisenstein and Pudovkin to cinematography, Meyerhold to theater, Shostakovich to music, and a galaxy of avant-garde artists to painting, but also Rodchenko, Ignatovich, Shaykhet, Shagin, Petrusov, Temin, and others to photojournalism and the photographic arts. Unfortunately, these names, with the exception of Aleksandr Rodchenko, are not as well known in world photography as they deserve to be.

The war, moreover, multiplied this list, which grew to include Baltermants, Garanin, Tarasevich, Khaldey, Arkashev, Trakhman, and many others. To some extent, they are represented in the pages of this book, but in addition to them the reader will also see here the photographs of authors whose names are not known even to the experts on Soviet war photography.

The supply of photographs of the last war is virtually inexhaustible. Each new decade separating us from the victorious year of 1945 uncovers new photographic subjects. Evidently this inexhaustibility is but one of many phenomena of the documentary art of photography, for which the criteria of value—the coefficient of authenticity and the quality of emotional force—change in the minds of each new generation. For the Soviet people, though, there is one inarguable constant throughout this photochronicle: the antiwar essence in its sympathy for the war's victims and its reverence for those who in Russia's difficult time upheld liberty and independence.

The first stills of the war toll like a dirge, an indictment of fascism and its savage nature. Fugitives on the roads, destroyed cities and villages, women and children victimized by bombs, churches blown up, earth shelled to pieces: these pictures, in many instances, were created by the same authors who, on the virtual eve of the war, celebrated the peaceful life of the country in the most optimistic of major chords. Does such a metamorphosis perhaps bear witness only to the highest professionalism of reporters who "can do everything"? No, to make that assertion means to cast doubt on the sincerity of the authors and to represent them merely as registrars and witnesses to events. This would be an insulting falsehood. The photoreporters at the front were participants and, in many cases, victims of the war. They fulfilled their civic and soldierly duty. Many of them were awarded orders and medals not only for their "main work" but also for their direct participation in heavy battles, when they were forced to take a submachine gun instead of a camera into their hands and stand in formation, fly in military airplanes as gunners and radio men, carry the wounded from the battlefield, and take part in guerrilla raids against the enemy's rear line.

Among the photographs of the first, severest months of the war—the months of retreat, followed by counterstrikes and the liberation of temporarily occupied populated areas—are many masterpieces of photojournalism. The most famous are "Sorrow" by Dmitri Baltermants and "Zoya" by Sergei Strunnikov. The first captures the execution by gunfire of the peaceful inhabitants outside Kerch, and the second has as its subject the tragic death of the guerrilla heroine Zoya Kosmodemyanskaya at the hands of the fascist butchers near Moscow. These stills, with their phenomenal qualities, cannot leave the viewer indifferent. With special conviction and undeniability they uphold the truth that the art of photography, in its best examples, possesses tremendous strength of artistic generalization while remaining simultaneously a documentary, spontaneous witness to a fact or event.

The legendary war correspondent Robert Capa maintained that if a photographer failed to take a good picture it meant that he was not close enough. The most effective stills of the war are convincing proof of this. It is not difficult to imagine how close Ivan Shagin was to the hero of his photograph "The political commander continues the fight." Just by being in on the attack and alongside soldiers running toward the enemy's trenches, Anatoli Garanin was able to get his picture "Death of a soldier."

Among the photographs of Soviet authors represented on these pages, not all, to be sure, can be considered masterpieces of photoreportage. The goal of this book, however, is not to present a collection of masterpieces. What is important is to give an overall view of war and a conceptual relationship to its events and the people who became its victims and heroes. In order to comprehend and give meaning to this concept—by no means born of today's intellectual and theoretical arguments, but on the battlefields—it is imperative to look very closely at the faces of the actors in the war and at the character of their performance, if it may be expressed in such a way. Then the truth that the war was *popular* will become clear. Its heroes are its toilers who, under the conditions, carried out the most difficult and dangerous work on earth. They never thought of themselves as supermen in military pursuits, seekers of military success, or "understudies" of figures from stereotypical blockbuster war films. These people remained unchanged in their high morality, even in the situations when their fate and that of their families was decided, as well as in the role of the victors entering Germany to requite the perpetrators of the war. Between the quiet conviction of the artilleryman Kavun in the photograph by Vasili Arkashev (Kavun subsequently died in battle, like many other people in these stills) and the joyful weeping of veterans whose return from the war Georgi Petrusov photographed at Moscow's Byelorusskiy Station, there is an interval of four blood-soaked years. But even in this interval there were happy moments. One need only look at the photographs that show the inhabitants of Eastern European countries, liberated from fascist invaders, greeting the Soviet soldiers.

Many examples of the high professional mastery and involvement of Soviet reporters could be given, but we shall confine ourselves to only one of them. When the Victory banner was hoisted above the Reichstag in conquered Berlin, Viktor Temin photographed the banner from an airplane, flew to Moscow of his own will, and on the following day returned to Berlin with bundles of *Pravda* in which his unique photo, entered into the history of war photojournalism, was published.

The stills of Mark Redkin and Aleksandr Ustinov, witnesses to the meeting of the allies—Soviet and American soldiers at the Elbe—occupy a special place in the photochronicles of war. The warmth and lyricism of these photos are in complete semantic harmony with this event, which to this day remains a symbol of friendship and unique protest against all wars of every kind.

Soviet photoreporters were witnesses to and participants in the military actions of the Soviet armed forces against militaristic Japan. Photos relating the destruction of the Kwantung Army and the signing of Japan's unconditional surrender have also entered into the photochronicles of war.

Among the many outstanding American masters of war photoreportage there are a number of reporters who were present at many different wars. Recently the author of these lines conversed with one of them. Eddie Adams took photographs in twelve (!) wars, winning the most prestigious awards for his masterpieces. He spoke with satisfaction about how, in his opinion, the photoreportage from Vietnam helped to end the war in that region of the world. All this is worthy of respect, but obviously the difference between the works of the Soviet war reporters and those of reporters who witnessed many wars lies precisely in the fact that the Soviet journalists were in one war—the Great Patriotic War—and were not only witnesses of but participants in this just and popular war. This is the general context of Soviet war photojournalism, in which its patriotic, antiwar and humanistic tendencies are found.

Perhaps the assertion that wars are not photographed for history is more than doubtful. Perhaps the most antimilitaristic genetic code is instilled in the up-to-the-minute World War II stills created by Soviet and American reporters and, if unlocked, can help the people of our planet prevent World War III, a nuclear war that threatens to destroy all mankind.

Of War and Pictures

by David E. Scherman

On a calm, sunny South Atlantic noon in April 1941, before either the United States of America or the Union of Soviet Socialist Republics had entered World War II, the captain of the German raider *Atlantis* was preparing to scuttle with sea mines the neutral Egyptian passenger ship *Zam Zam*. Somewhat to his embarrassment, he had shelled and captured the same vessel early that morning, killing one elderly nonbelligerent North Carolinian and dumping 138 assorted nonbelligerent American missionaries and their wives and children into the water—and only partially in lifeboats, since his guns had destroyed many of them. The German captain's aide, an avid amateur photographer with many sinking snaps to his credit, said to a *Life* photographer who had been fished out of the water with the *Zam Zam* survivors: "We usually stand up here for the nicest pictures of the victims watching their ship go down." The photographer politely stood where he was told and clicked away, having already secreted in a tube of toothpaste in his pocket a roll of film containing the raider's profile, photographed at dawn from a lifeboat—a picture whose appearance in the June 23, 1941 issue of *Life* occasioned the sighting, identification, and sinking of *Atlantis* by a British cruiser a few months later.

The incidents of the two pictures—one designed to *tell a story* and shot from the relative safety of a warship's deck, the other an attempt to *record an instant* of history while standing dry-mouthed and terror-stricken in a swamped lifeboat and foolishly worrying about how one would ever cover the 600 miles to Africa—say quite a lot about modern combat photography, the subject of this book.

By the 1930s, when the seeds of World War II were being sown in Europe, Asia, and Africa, war photography had leapt a long way from the days when Matthew Brady virtually suspended American Civil War hostilities to make his historical, lengthy time exposures. The new miniature cameras, fast film, and resulting "candid," available light techniques had created modern photojournalism, the perfect medium for witnessing the political impact, the deeds of heroism, the hatred and terror, the destruction, the compassion, the hideous artistry of modern warfare, which was another technological triumph. Alfred Eisenstaedt, to many the father of the new photojournalism and surely its most durable practitioner (he turned 90 in 1988), used the new methods to portray the architects of Fascism and Nazism in Europe and to cover Mussolini's war in Ethiopia. Robert Capa, possibly the greatest chronicler of war since Brady, went to China and Spain, test tube for World War II. Armed with the new techniques but still practicing them in peace, their counterparts in the Soviet Union—Georgi Zelma, Dmitri Baltermants, Yevgeni Khaldey, Sergei Strunnikov, to name a few among many—and in the United States—the budding Army Signal Corps, the press associations, and, most importantly, the 25-person team of the new picture weekly *Life*, the first and probably the last medium of its kind—were poised to cover the biggest, bloodiest, most dramatic continuous event of modern times when Hitler attacked Russia in June and the Japanese struck Hawaii in December 1941.

And so, to revert to the maritime anecdote above, war photography with all its technical advances was seen to involve *both* the seizure of an exact instant under fire, as in Anatoli Garanin's incredible "Death of a Soldier," and thoughtful, tenderly composed storytelling, as in Khaldey's troubled Muscovites or Bill Vandivert's classic of an old Londoner warming her hands on a convenient incendiary bomb just dropped by the Luftwaffe.

Half a century after the experience of the war's insanity, one finds it difficult to recall precisely what our motivation for reporting it was. For our part on the *Life* team, we followed orders to go out and produce meaningful pictures, and I'm certain the orders to our Soviet allies were not much different. Beyond duty, there were doubtlessly pride, ambition, and artistic professionalism, but I have to agree with Grigori Chudakov when he says that it would be insulting to ascribe the pictures in this startling book only to journalistic professionalism.

That the Soviet armed forces (and their combat-photographer companions) fought a war different from that fought by their American counterparts is beyond question. The one was a monumental (and victorious, thank goodness) struggle against an enemy who wrought satanic devastation on a people, their land, and the fabric of their society in a way that Americans—except for the shock of Pearl Harbor—never really felt, despite the infinite number of other American tragedies that ensued. Indeed, future historians will be hard put to explain satisfactorily why the average American G.I. (with scarcely a thought in his mind about regaining world capitalist hegemony) fought as well as he did. Some historians, ironically, will attribute it to ideology, a quality that Yanks are supposed to have in short supply. I might go along with that idea if ideology connotes an abiding hatred of obvious evil, a heroic willingness to fight it at any cost, and a sense of human compassion. No lack of bravery, anger, or compassion existed among the soldiers, sailors, and airmen I knew, or among the combat photojournalists who traveled with and, occasionally, ahead of them. (For instance, Eugene Smith was first wounded when he was out ahead of his patrol pointing his camera back at their advance.) In terms of pure anger, one thinks of Bob Landry's picture of a Cherbourg collaborator. And in terms of compassion, we remember Ralph Morse, whose French *poilu* regaining his motherland is quite moving. When Morse was sunk in the Pacific off Guadalcanal (losing all his film, sadly), he kept a life-jacketless shipmate afloat for six hours until help came. Surviving that, he landed in Normandy on D-Day and was seen shortly afterwards by a fellow reporter not taking pictures but carrying wounded G.I.s out of the wreckage of Saint-Lô.

There was no shortage of bravery or commitment, but a peculiar aspect of the U.S. journalist's bravery existed because of his power of choice. As Capa put it: "Having the freedom to choose his spot and being allowed to be a coward and not be executed for it is the war correspondent's torture. He has his stake—his life—in his own hands, and he can put it on this horse or that horse, or he can put it back in his pocket at the very last minute." Once, as a paratrooper was dropping out of a C-47 over Sicily, he shouted back at Capa: "I don't like your job—it's too dangerous!" And hours before he was hit on Okinawa, Gene Smith spoke of an infantryman he had chosen to cover: "I envied him. He had been *ordered* to move up. I could drop out. Now he had only fear. I had fear and the recurrent thought, 'What the hell am I doing here?'"

What indeed were *we* doing there? We the white-hats were there, and so were our white-hatted Soviet colleagues, because of three black-hatted megalomaniacs who thought they could take over the assets of what they considered the world's "lesser peoples," and by force. If one prefers to call them "fascist butchers," as Chudakov does, that's all right by me. It has a nice ring to it, even today.

So despite their "different" wars, the motivations of the two allies were not really different at all, nor are the results of their four-year ordeal: the pictures. You will notice that when you see them side by side. They were taken in fear and anger, some out of humanity, some for the artistic joy that they brought to the takers (no matter how horrendous the subject), some because the historical urgency of the moment could not be denied. And some, I am certain, were taken with a deep feeling of humor, despite the seriousness of the war. It is hard, even after all this time, for me to forget the joking camaraderie between the American and Russian soldiers joining up on the Elbe at Torgau. Hardly anyone was sober. And those of us who were in Paris in 1946 affectionately remember when Yevgeni Khaldey (he decided we should call him George when he hated our pronunciation of Yevgeni) arrived to report the Foreign Ministers' Conference; the evenings when he and our *Life* "family"—Ralph and Ruth Morse, Robert Capa, Gjon Mili, Elmer Lower, Rosemarie Redlich, Barbara O'Connor, among others—would share a meal and swap the inevitable wartime lies were warm occasions. This was just about the time when such meetings were already beginning to be looked upon as "fraternizing with the enemy." We were still in the clear, but Yevgeni had to eat two dinners—one at the Soviet delegation commissary and the other with us at the Allied mess. Perhaps *glasnost* and *perestroika,* properly managed by both sides of the slowly rising Iron Curtain, will render the term "allies" more meaningful than did the fortuitous state of affairs when we both went after a common enemy. For Yevgeni and his confreres no less, I am sure, than for me and mine, that peaceful prospect is profoundly to be hoped for.

David E. Scherman (left) poses with a Soviet soldier and fellow photographer
Johnny Florea (right) at the Elbe River, 1945. Photograph by Lee Miller.

ALLIES

Yevgeni Khaldey

On a Moscow street the first day of the war. 1941

Arkadi Shaykhet

"Mayakovskaya" metro station, Moscow. During an air raid. 1941

William Vandivert

Trafalgar Square, London. Hand-warming over an incendiary bomb. 1940

Mikhail Kalashnikov

Parade on Red Square. November 1941

Aleksandr Ustinov

Moscow volunteers—fighting men of a work battalion. 1941

Thomas McAvoy

Washington, D.C. Machine guns atop the Commerce Department. 1942

Boris Kudoyarov

Leningrad. First day of the war. 1941

Alfred Eisenstaedt

New York City. Penn Station farewells. 1943

Robert Diament

A sailor of the Northern Fleet. 1944

Vasili Arkashev

Artilleryman Ivan Kavun. 1941

Emmanuil Yevzerikhin

Scout. 1942

United States Army Signal Corps

Germany. U.S. infantrymen's first hot meal in two weeks. December 1944

Mark Markov-Grinberg

Oath of war. 1943

United States Army Signal Corps

Normandy. By the Chalk Cliff. June 1944

Iosif Fetisov

He remained in formation. 1942

Robert Capa

Arras, France. Mohawk-style paratroopers target the Rhine. March 1945

Georgi Lipskerov

Czechoslovakia. Let the soldiers sleep a little. 1945

Robert Capa
Wesel, Germany.
Germans shell an
American-held farm.
1945

Yevgeni Khaldey

Outside Murmansk.

1942

David E. Scherman

Munich, Germany. Looting. 1945

Robert Capa

Berlin. Black-market carts. August 1945

Mark Redkin

Home again. 1943

Arkadi Shaykhet

In a liberated village. 1944

Dmitri Baltermants

Sorrow. 1942

Vasili Arkashev

Victims of the fascist terror. 1943

United States Army Signal Corps

Italy. A cave-dweller found by Nazis. 1943

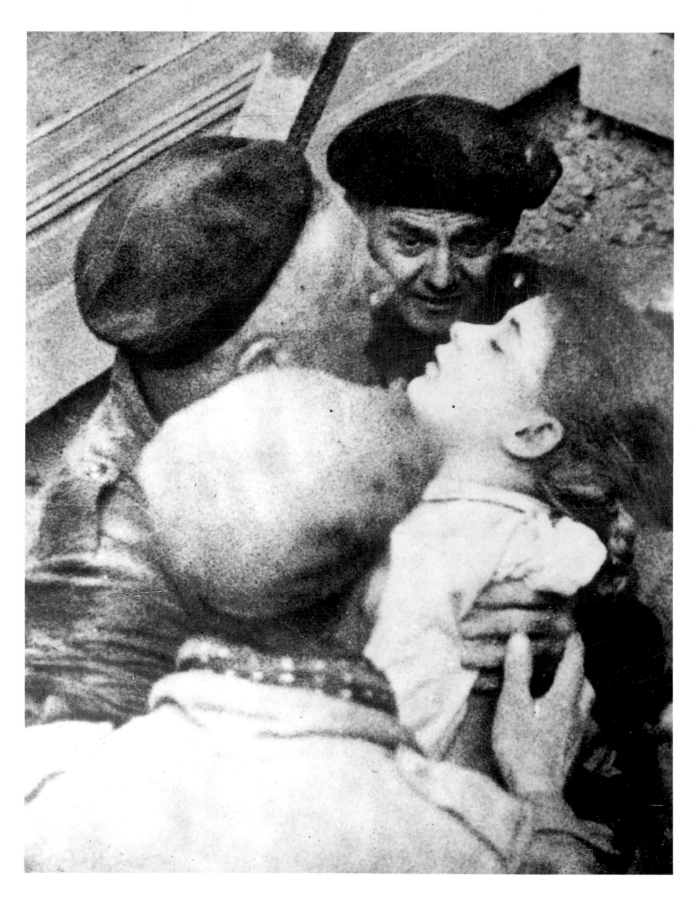

United States Army Signal Corps

Bombing victim.

Mikhail Savin

At the site of a fire. 1943

Mikhail Kalashnikov

Captured Germans. 1943

Yakov Davidzon

The legendary guerrilla commander Sidor Kovpak. 1943

Yakov Davidzon

Milk for wounded guerrillas. 1942

Ralph Morse

Normandy. A Frenchman on French soil. 1944

Bob Landry

Renner, Brittany. Cornered collaborator. August 1944

David E. Scherman

The South Atlantic. A German raider sinks the Egyptian Zam Zam. *April 1941*

Dmitri Kessel

The Florida coast. Torpedoed allied tanker. 1942

United States Army Signal Corps

U.S. forces en route to Morocco. November 1942

Vsevolod Tarasevich

Assault on the city of Narva. 1942

Vsevolod Tarasevich

Crossing the Neva. 1941

United States Army Signal Corps

Salerno, Sicily. Warships firing on aircraft. September 1943

United States Army Signal Corps

The North Atlantic. Winter's assault on a U.S. warship. December 1943

Robert Diament

After the landing of troops. 1944

Robert Diament

The big guns open fire. 1944

Robert Diament

Nurse Nina Bezraeva (she saved sixty wounded sailors). 1944

United States Army Signal Corps

Oberwesel, Germany. U.S. troops cross the Rhine. March 1945

Ivan Shagin

Chelyabinsk. At a weapons factory. 1942

Vsevolod Tarasevich

In the shop of a Leningrad factory. 1942

Eliot Elisofon

San Diego, California. B240 assembly. 1942

Peter Stackpole

Texas. A student solos. 1943

Aleksandr Dmitriev

Fighter pilot Fyodor Khimich, hero of the Soviet Union. 1943

Viktor Polikhanov

Before taking off. 1944

Robert Diament

Transport of torpedoes. 1944

Robert Capa

Chelveston, England. A belly landing. November 1942

United States Army Signal Corps

Germany. Awaiting Nazi strafers after an aerial dogfight. 1944

Robert Diament

Torpedo carriers in flight. 1944

Kazimir Lishko

Fascist bombers over Kiev. June 1941

United States Army Signal Corps

U.S. bombers approach Berlin.

Aleksandr Dmitriev

An assault on the enemy's position. 1944

Margaret Bourke-White

Bombed airfield. 1944

United States Army Signal Corps

Germany. A U.S. P-47 strikes an enemy ammunition truck.

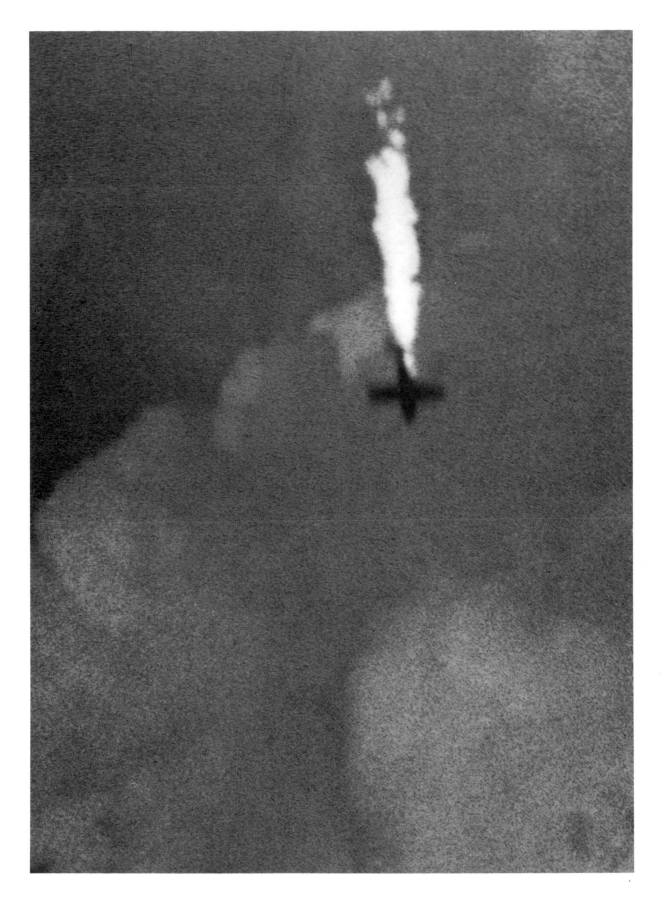

Ivan Shagin

Fascist airplane shot down by Soviet ace Ivan Kozhedub. 1943

Dmitri Baltermants

Attack. 1941

Vsevolod Tarasevich

Leningrad front. Beginning of the offensive. 1943

Mark Markov-Grinberg

For the Motherland! 1943

Anatoli Garanin

Death of a soldier. 1942

Aleksandr Ustinov

Battalion attacking. 1944

Anatoli Garanin

Battle near Kharkov. 1942

Robert Capa

Belgium. Help on the way for encircled American units
in Bastogne. December 1944

Vsevolod Tarasevich

Salvo of "Katyush" rockets on the avenues

of approach to Vyborg. 1944

Anatoli Garanin

Attack outside Rzhev. 1942

Aleksandr Ustinov

Against the enemy tanks! 1944

Robert Diament

Machine gunners change position. 1944

Margaret Bourke-White

The Italian front. Night artillery barrage. Spring 1944

Peter Stackpole

West coast preparedness. 1941

United States Army Signal Corps

Sindorf, Germany. A U.S. cinematographer films the
Nazi destruction of German homes. 1945

United States Army Signal Corps
Loiano, Italy. German shell attack. 1945

United States Army Signal Corps
Cherbourg, France. American advance. 1944

George Silk

Germany. Second Armored Division tanks near the Rhine. March 1945

Robert Capa

Germany. Jumping on the Rhine. March 1945

Georgi Zelma

Stalingrad. Common grave. 1942

United States Army Signal Corps

Snowstorm.

Robert Capa

Wesel, Germany. Wounded paratrooper. March 1945

Ivan Shagin

The political commander continues the fight. 1943

Robert Capa

Palermo, Sicily. A German found by Americans. 1943

Robert Capa

Salerno, Sicily. British surgeons work in a church. 1943

Vasili Arkashev

Dancing during a break. 1943

Yakov Khalil

"Nocturne." 1943

Dmitri Kessel

Pin-ups. 1944

Aldgate, London. Children's theater. 1943

United States Army Signal Corps

Carentan, France. For a German retreat, a U.S. sendoff. 1944

Emmanuil Yevzerikhin

Stand to the last man! 1943

Aleksandr Ustinov

Tanks go into battle. 1941

Vladimir Yudin

Mortarman. 1943

Dmitri Baltermants

Crossing the Oder River. 1944

Robert Capa

Bastogne, Belgium. The Battle of the Bulge tanks. December 1944

Sergei Strunnikov

Scouts of the Moscow sky. 1941

Aleksandr Ustinov

Fire on Berlin! 1945

Georgi Zelma

The battle for Krivoi Rog. 1943

Aleksandr Ustinov

Soviet tanks head towards Berlin. 1945

Izrael Ozerskiy

A soldier's work. 1944

Dmitri Baltermants

On a military road. 1941

United States Army Signal Corps

Malmedy, Belgium. A Belgian victim of Nazi rapists. January 1945

Sergei Strunnikov

Zoya (guerrilla heroine Zoya Kosmodemyanskaya). 1941

Ivan Shagin

Berlin. He got his deserts. May 1945

Vsevolod Tarasevich

Leningrad. Victim of artillery shelling. 1941

George Silk

Roer River, Germany. Death of a G.I. 1945

Johnny Florea

Nazi murder of a captured U.S. convoy. February 1945

United States Army Signal Corps

Malmedy, Belgium. Surrender to Nazis brought death. January 1945

United States Army Signal Corps

Houffalise, Belgium. Advancing G.I., fallen enemies. 1945

Robert Capa

Bastogne, Belgium. The Battle of the Bulge. December 1944

Robert Capa

Wesel, Germany. American paratrooper. March 1945

Robert Capa

Leipzig. American machine gunner. April 1945

Margaret Bourke-White

Leipzig. Nazi suicides. April 1945

Vsevolod Tarasevich

Leningrad. Artillery shelling. 1941

Anatoli Garanin

Isaakievski Cathedral, during the blockade of Leningrad. 1942

Boris Kudoyarov

In defense of Leningrad.

Georgi Zelma
Stalingrad. Street battle. 1942

134

Robert Capa
Leipzig.
Street fighting.
April 1945

Georgi Zelma
Stalingrad.
Battle for a floor.
1942

Emmanuil Yevzerikhin

Stalingrad. Railway station platform. 1942

Arkadi Shaykhet

Kiev. The first day of liberation. 1943

Viktor Temin

Assault on Berlin. 1945

David E. Scherman

Nuremburg. Americans search for prisoners. April 1945

United States Army Signal Corps
The Third Reich in 1945.

United States Army Signal Corps

German street. Spring 1945

United States Army Signal Corps
The liberation of Paris. August 1944

United States Army Signal Corps

Place de la Concorde, Paris. Nazi snipers attack

as Allied troops arrive. August 1944

William Vandivert

London, 1940

Arkadi Shaykhet

Profaned by the fascists. 1942

United States Army Signal Corps

Cologne, Germany. A cathedral spared by Allied bombers. February 1945

United States Army Signal Corps

Bombing Nuremburg. April 1945

Margaret Bourke-White

Hitler's legacy to Nuremburg. May 1945

Georgi Petrusov

The Reichstag is taken! 1945

Viktor Temin

Berlin. Victory banner above the Reichstag. May 1945

William Vandivert

Berlin. Soviet graffiti on the Reichstag. 1945

Robert Capa

The English Channel. A barge to Normandy. June 1944

Robert Capa

The Normandy coast. D-Day. June 1944

Robert Capa

Omaha Beach. June 1944

United States Army Signal Corps

Northern France. A flood of reinforcements. June 1944

United States Army Signal Corps

Southern France. A flurry of parachutes. August 1944

Robert Capa

Normandy. Local witnesses to war. June 1944

Mark Markov-Grinberg

This cannot be forgotten (death camp Stutthof). 1945

Margaret Bourke-White

Germany. Site of a bombing. 1945

United States Army Signal Corps

Mauthasen, Austria. Spanish Loyalist prisoners
welcome the U.S. Third Army. May 1945

Vladimir Yudin

Auschwitz. January 1945

United States Army Signal Corps

Mauthasen, Austria. Liberation. May 1945

United States Army Signal Corps

Ohrdruf, Germany. Eisenhower, Bradley, and Patton
view slain prisoners. April 1945

United States Army Signal Corps

Estedt, Germany. Graves for murdered prisoners. May 1945

United States Army Signal Corps

Solengen, Germany. Allied reburial of Gestapo victims. May 1945

Aleksandr Ustinov

Meeting the first American soldiers at the Elbe River. 1945

Mark Redkin

Meeting at the Elbe River. Cossacks and Americans. 1945

United States Army Signal Corps

A shared triumph.

Aleksandr Ustinov

Meeting at the Elbe. Friendly conversation between
Soviet and American officers. 1945

United States Army Signal Corps

Apollensdorf, Germany. Allies exchange congratulations. April 1945

United States Army Signal Corps

The Elbe River, Germany. A sign of victory. April 1945

Yevgeni Kopyt

Meeting at the Elbe. Allies. April 1945

Robert Capa

Germany. Price settlement over an ally's wristwatch. 1945

United States Army Signal Corps

Torgau, Germany. Toasting the U.S. and Red armies. April 1945

United States Army Signal Corps

An American–Russian embrace. April 1945

United States Army Signal Corps

The Big Three: Stalin, Roosevelt, Churchill.

Samari Gurari

At the Crimean conference. 1945

Yevgeni Khaldey

At the round table of the Berlin Conference. 1945

United States Army Signal Corps

Berlin. Stalin and Truman pose. July 1945

Ivan Shagin

The first traffic controller of Berlin. 1945

Ivan Shagin

Salvo on the roof of the Reichstag. 1945

United States Army Signal Corps

Mauthasen, Austria. End of a concentration camp. May 1945

Sergei Loskutov

Victory parade, Moscow. Fascist banners are laid at Lenin's mausoleum. 1945

Georgi Zelma

Stalingrad is liberated! 1943

Robert Capa

Monreale, Sicily. The Yanks take Palermo. July 1943

Yevgeni Khaldey

The inhabitants of Belgrade greet the Soviet soldiers-liberators. 1944

United States Army Signal Corps

Paris. Champs-Elysées victory parade, 1944

Dmitri Baltermants

Captured Germans on the streets of Moscow. 1944

Yevgeni Khaldey

Rejoicing in Bulgaria. 1944

Georgi Petrusov

The signing of unconditional surrender. 1945

Georgi Petrusov

Meeting of the first echelon of victors. 1945

Georgi Petrusov

Moscow. Victory salute. May 1945

Gordon Coster

Chicago. V-J Day. August 1945

PHOTO CREDITS

The publisher gratefully acknowledges VAAP, the Soviet copyright agency, for its assistance in obtaining and releasing for republication the work of the Soviet photographers included in ALLIES.

p. 17: William Vandivert, *Life* magazine © 1940, Time Inc.

p. 20: Thomas McAvoy, *Life* magazine © 1942, Time Inc.

p. 22: Alfred Eisenstaedt, *Life* magazine © Time Inc.

p. 26, 28: National Archives.

p. 30, 32–33: © Robert Capa—Magnum Photos Inc.

p. 36: David E. Scherman, *Life* magazine © 1945, Time Inc.

p. 37: © Robert Capa—Magnum Photos Inc.

p. 42, 43: National Archives.

p. 48: Ralph Morse, *Life* magazine © 1944, 1972, Time Inc.

p. 49: Bob Landry, *Life* magazine © Time Inc.

pp. 50–51: David E. Scherman, *Life* magazine © 1941, Time Inc.

p. 52: Dmitri Kessel, *Life* magazine © 1942, Time Inc.

p. 53, 56, 57, 61: National Archives.

p. 64: Eliot Elisofon, *Life* magazine © Time Inc.

p. 65: Peter Stackpole, *Life* magazine © 1943, Time Inc.

p. 69: © Robert Capa—Magnum Photos Inc.

p. 70, 73: National Archives.

p. 75: Margaret Bourke-White, *Life* magazine © 1944, Time Inc.

p. 76: National Archives.

p. 84: © Robert Capa—Magnum Photos Inc.

p. 89: Margaret Bourke-White, *Life* magazine © 1945, Time Inc.

p. 90: Peter Stackpole, *Life* magazine © Time Inc.

p. 91, 92, 93: National Archives.

p. 94: George Silk, *Life* magazine © Time, Inc.

p. 95: © Robert Capa—Magnum Photos Inc.

p. 97: National Archives.

p. 98, 100, 101: © Robert Capa—Magnum Photos Inc.

p. 104: Dmitri Kessel, *Life* magazine © 1944, Time Inc.

p. 105: Courtesy *Life* magazine © 1943, Time Inc.

p. 106: National Archives.

p. 111: © Robert Capa—Magnum Photos Inc.

p. 118: National Archives.

p. 122: George Silk, *Life* magazine © 1945, Time Inc.

p. 123: Johnny Florea, *Life* magazine © 1945, Time Inc.

p. 124, 125: National Archives.

p. 126, 127, 128: © Robert Capa—Magnum Photos Inc.

p. 129: Margaret Bourke-White, *Life* magazine © 1945, Time Inc.

pp. 134–35: © Robert Capa—Magnum Photos Inc.

p. 141: David E. Scherman, *Life* magazine © Time Inc.

p. 142, 143, 144, 145: National Archives.

p. 146: William Vandivert, *Life* magazine © 1940, Time Inc.

p. 148, 149: National Archives.

p. 150: Margaret Bourke-White, *Life* magazine © Time Inc.

p. 153: William Vandivert, *Life* magazine © Time Inc.

p. 154: National Archives.

p. 155, 156: © Robert Capa—Magnum Photos Inc.

p. 157, 158: National Archives.

p. 159: © Robert Capa—Magnum Photos Inc.

p. 161: Margaret Bourke-White, *Life* magazine © Time Inc.

p. 162, 164, 165, 166, 167, 170, 172, 173: National Archives.

p. 175: © Robert Capa—Magnum Photos Inc.

p. 178, 181, 184: National Archives.

p. 187: © Robert Capa—Magnum Photos Inc.

p. 189: National Archives.

p. 196: Tony Linck, *Life* magazine © Time Inc.

p. 199: Gordon Coster, *Life* magazine © Time Inc.